Why Believe in life after death?

Robert Dawson

Illustrations by
Alice Englander

HUNT& THORPE

contents

special activities

Activities for you to do are shown by the following symbols:

from the Bible...

Borrow a Bible or get one out of the library, and find out more on the subject in question.

check it out...

Don't just take our word for it – investigate for yourself, and see what you find!

for you to try...

You might need a pen and paper where you see this symbol, or there may be an experiment to do.

talk about it...

If you have some friends or grown-ups with you, talk about how you feel about what you've read.

Introduction

It's frightening to think about dying. It's not just fear of something new happening, it's everything else that's connected with it. When we mention death, lots of questions come to our minds.

Above: As we get older the idea that we will die becomes more familiar.

- Will it hurt me to die?
- Will I ever see the people I love again?
- What will happen after I'm dead?
- Will I see nasty things?
- Who will look after me?
- Where is it?
- How do I 'get' to wherever I'm going?
- If it doesn't involve 'going' somewhere, what is there instead?

Finding answers to questions like these isn't easy. This book tries to answer your questions.

The *Bible* tells us lots of things about what will happen after we are dead. Many Christians believe that the *Bible* is God's word, so whatever it teaches must be right. Other people argue that holy books, including the *Bible*, could be wrong in what they say. This

book tries to explore whether you can believe what the *Bible* tells us about life after death.

There are other ways to explore ideas about life after death. These ways may conflict with or agree with the teaching of the *Bible*. For instance, some people actually claim to have been to heaven. This book describes their experiences, too.

So here goes.

Right: Gravestones and other memorials help keep people who have died alive in our minds.

Part 1

The 'what happened?' game

The whole of this section is a mystery game for you to solve. Can you work out what happened? See what you can remember about it? And who was involved? The police will want to interview you, because you are a very important witness. Don't forget a thing! It could be vital to catch the criminals, if there are any!

for you to try...

One day, on your way somewhere in the car, you see something odd…

For the first part of the game, you can have exactly two minutes (not even one extra second). Get a watch or timer with a second hand ready. When you've read this box, you'll be told to turn to the next page and examine the picture carefully, deciding what is happening and who is involved. The car in the foreground is the one in which you are a passenger so you needn't remember anything about that. After two minutes of looking, come back to this page.

It is now later in the day. The police have interviewed every witness except you. You were the only person in your car who saw what happened (so if there are a group of you, this part has to be done individually).

In a moment, a policeman will show you pictures of people at the scene. Some of them witnessed the crime, but there is a doubt about who was involved and who wasn't.

The man in the entrance to the bank, who is the manager ❾, has told the police that a masked man came into the bank with a gun. He held up a cashier ❹ and demanded a bag of money. As he ran back out of the bank, he pushed aside the lady in the suit ❺, who courageously ran after him. She was joined by another man (the third runner) ❽. He tried to give chase, too.

The lady in the suit accidentally banged into the old lady ❻ and knocked her down.

Above: The police have assembled the pictures of everyone involved in the incident.

She had to stop to help the old lady.

Meanwhile, the man who had held up the bank leapt into the car with its three doors open. He and the driver slammed two doors, slamming the other as they drove off at high speed. The police are satisfied Mr Cuthbert ❽ was an innocent bystander who tried to catch the robbers, but was too late. They know Mrs Jones ❼ is totally innocent, too.

Your task is to decide who the robber is. All the indentikits are numbered. Write down the numbers of anyone or everyone who you think was involved in the crime. The car driver ❶ and the gunman ❷ are two of the people shown. Were they the only criminals? Can you explain how the robbery and the getaway took place?

The answer is given on the next page.

answer

(Do not read this until you have finished the previous page.)

Here is what really happened. Did you manage to work it out?

The gunman had accomplices. As he left the bank, he pushed the bag of money at the woman in the suit. She ran after him as if she was chasing him. She banged into the old lady, who was really another gang member, and she hid the money in her shopping bag.

The actual gunman made off in the getaway car. At the last minute, the woman in the suit decided it would look better if she helped the old lady.

How did you do?

Things aren't always as they seem. We don't always see the whole picture.

Life after death is very like that, too. People who say they've experienced it may not be explaining what actually happened, only what they think happened.

We're all only human, so it's possible that anything involving what people witness may not be quite as it seems. Or it could be absolutely spot on. We've no way of telling.

Above: As soon as a baby is born, the hospital nurses put on a wristband with his or her name on it.

Part 2

I know because I know

What is your first name? Where did it come from?
It was probably given to you by your parents. As a newborn baby, you had no choice in the matter. Maybe you're happy with being
Jack or Lucy or whoever, or maybe you wish you were called something different.

talk about it...

Say your name out loud. It doesn't matter whether you do this alone or in a group. Now think or talk about how you know what your name is.

When you are a grown-up, you can change your name if you really want to, but for the time being you're stuck with it. It's something you've probably had all your life. You know it without even thinking.

If someone asks you your name, you don't sit there fumbling:

"Oh, er, just a minute! Let me think… I should know it. Er…"

And if someone came along and said, "No, that's not your real name. Yours is Fred (or Mavis) Midget-Gem," you wouldn't believe them. You'd want a lot of proof.

Right: We all know how pain feels even though it's hard to describe.

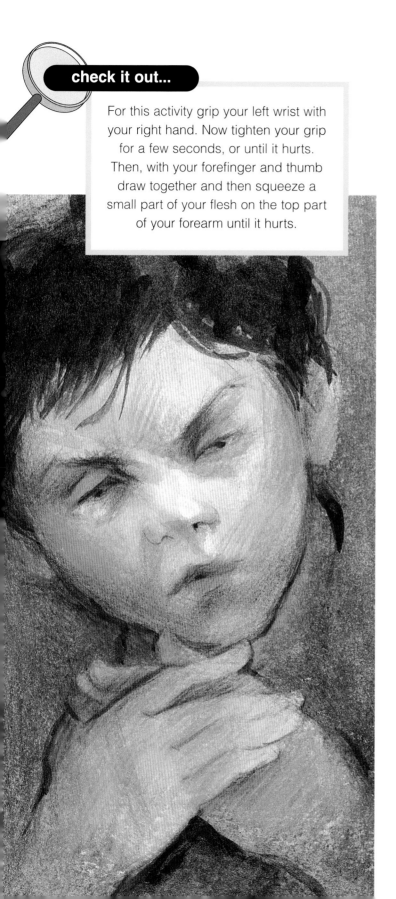

Pinching yourself hurts, of course. What's more, you knew it would. At some time in your life, you discovered that it's possible to feel pain when something nasty happens. I don't know how you discovered that, and perhaps you don't either. Maybe you touched something hot, or fell, or trapped your fingers in a door. But you know that you can feel pain.

When you were little, people probably warned you about things:

"Don't touch that! It's hot!"

"Be careful, you'll cut yourself."

"Mind your fingers."

But some things we can only find out for ourselves. Like pricking yourself with the pin. Telling you wasn't enough. You had to find out for yourself.

You can't really describe the pain. But if you say "Ouch!", people know you're hurt.

We experience other things that we can't tell others about. We just have to assume that they have some idea of what we're going through. Dying is like that. It happens to everyone, so we know it will happen to us, too (probably not for a very long time). But no-one can actually tell us what it's like.

Well, that's not quite true. Some people have died and been brought back to life by expert doctors. They've been able to describe what happened. More about that soon.

Also, we can read about what happens in the *Bible* and other holy books. The *Bible* teaches that death isn't just an ending. Zap. It teaches that death is just a change and that there is something more to follow.

Part 3

A total blank

Humanists believe there's really nothing after we die. They think we simply cease to exist.

for you to try...

Let's pretend that a few minutes ago, a fairy – and no-one knows whether that fairy was good or bad – gave you a special present. For the next six hours you can have anything you want. Yes, anything!

You can only get things for yourself or for other people you know. After the six hours are up, no-one can take the things off you. You don't have to pay a penny.

What a present!

The only problem is, you can't actually magic things to you. You have to go and get them for yourself. If, for instance, you wanted to become a millionaire, you'd have to go and fetch the million from somewhere. Anywhere you think there might be a million. No-one will stop you. Just help yourself!

Perhaps you'd like some new clothes for yourself, for your mum or dad, or brother or sister. Where would you get some? You can have anything you want – the most expensive clothes in the world if you wish. How about some brand new designer clothes? Or maybe even a royal crown or two!

Or what about owning a famous footballer's complete kit? Or his car! Wouldn't your friends be jealous?

Make a list of all the things you'd get. They don't have to be in any special order. Talk about what's on your list and if others have done the same, talk about what's on theirs.

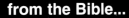
Left: Would having everything you want make you happy?

Above: If everyone could do whatever they wanted, more people would suffer than benefit.

What did you put down?

And more important, did you see the snag? If you can help yourself to anything you want and no-one can do anything about it, you can steal to your heart's content. It doesn't matter if other people suffer. It doesn't matter if we upset them, or make them sad or afraid.

If nothing happens to stop us, we can do anything we want – even nasty things.

Taking it one step further, if there's no life after death, it doesn't matter what you do in this life because there can be no come-back in heaven.

Of course, most humanists are good people, and live their lives well and honestly. They realise that evil deeds harm everyone.

But the danger of not believing in life after death is that nothing really matters any more. If we only relied on the laws of the land, many more people would do wrong things knowing there was a good chance they wouldn't be caught. They wouldn't care what happened to anyone else.

Part 4

What happened to Jesus?

If you know your Bible, *you'll remember how Jesus was crucified until he died, then buried in a cave. But all along, in his teachings to his followers, he'd said that he'd be resurrected.*

What does that word mean? Look it up in a dictionary if you're not sure. It will probably say something like, 'risen from the dead.' Which doesn't really help us to understand.

Throughout his life, Jesus made it clear many times that, on the third day after his death, he would rise from the grave, ascend into heaven, and be there with God. And he said that when they die those who followed him would also be in heaven with him.

Did it happen?

You can read about it for yourself in the New Testament of the *Bible*. But before you do, here's another activity for you to do.

for you to try...

Find an ordinary pack of playing cards. Take out any jokers – you won't need them.

Shuffle the pack well and place it face down on the table.

The next bit is hard. You have to pretend you don't know that a pack of cards has four suits (hearts, cubs, diamonds and spades).

Turn over the cards one at a time (turn them over from the top of the pack). Little by little, you'll notice that the same four shapes keep appearing on the cards.

When you get to the end of the pack, turn it over and go through again. This time, sort the cards into four piles – one for each suit. When all the cards are sorted, there will be 13 cards in each pile. Check this.

Check one of the suits. Starting with the ace, it goes through the numbers to 10, then there are three royal cards.

It's exactly the same in every suit.

So there are four piles of identically numbered cards, each with a different shape on them (their suit). Even if you had never seen playing cards before, you would soon work out there was a pattern to them.

If there is a pattern, it can, of course, be pure chance. But in the case of a pack of cards, there's so much of a pattern that someone must have designed them like that deliberately.

The order in which you turn them over is random, but the actual cards are deliberate and designed.

Left: Playing cards aren't random — they are designed to a pattern.

Now back to Jesus. Let's look at the evidence, as if it was being presented at a trial.

1. Jesus's body disappears from the cave.

2. Mary sees Jesus in the garden. She doesn't recognize him at once, so he must look different.

3. The disciples see Jesus on a mountain in Galilee and he speaks to them.

4. Two disciples meet Jesus on the road near Emmaus. They don't recognize him at first.

5. When they tell this to the other disciples, Jesus appears and eats with them.

6. A second time, Jesus appears in a locked room with the disciples. Thomas, who has doubts, touches Jesus's wounds.

7. Jesus meets the disciples on the shores of the Sea of Tiberias when they return with fish, and cooks breakfast for them.

Below: There's a pattern to the story of Jesus's resurrection, too.

What's your verdict?

If you were given evidence that someone had been seen by all these different people on all these occasions, would you believe they were really there?

The exact order in which these sightings of Jesus happened isn't known. In just the same way, you'll have memories of your life when you were a very young child, but you probably won't exactly remember exactly their order. But just as there's no question they happened to you, there's no question that Jesus was seen. Just because we weren't there to see him, doesn't mean it didn't happen. If we only relied on what we ourselves had seen, we wouldn't believe very much at all.

Would we?

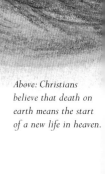

Part 5

What does the Bible say?

Life after death is often mentioned in the Bible. It comes in the letters of Paul and most of all in the teachings of Jesus in the Gospels of Matthew, Mark, Luke and John. The idea of life after death also comes in the Old Testament.

from the Bible...

Jesus said, 'There was a rich man, who was clothed in purple, and who feasted every day. And at his gate lay a poor man named Lazarus... The poor man died and was carried by the angels to Abraham's bosom. The rich man also died and was buried; and in Hades, being in torment, he lifted up his eyes and saw Abraham far off and Lazarus in his bosom. And he called out, Father Abraham, have mercy upon me and send Lazarus to dip the end of his finger in water and cool my tongue; for I am in anguish in this flame.' But Abraham said, Son, remember that you in your lifetime received your good things, and Lazarus in like manner evil things; but now he is comforted here, and you are in anguish.'
(Luke 16: 19 - 25)

The Gospel of John is clear that because of Jesus, everyone will be resurrected – that is, that we will die, physically, but will then go to a new life in heaven.

This certainty is found in several other books of the *Bible*. St Paul talks about it in his letters (see 1 *Corinthians* 15:54 and *Romans* 8:38-39). In these books of the *Bible*, it is often stressed that this is because of the covenant (promise) between God and people who believe.

Above: Christians believe that death on earth means the start of a new life in heaven.

for you to try...

Imagine you are starting a club or youth group. Write down the rules you'd make about who could be members. The other rules don't matter for the time being. Think, will there be people of particular ages, beliefs, outlooks? Will your club be limited to people in your own town or village or church? How will you decide who can be a member?

Left: Do you think that a club should have different sorts of people in it — like a pick and mix selection?

One of the problems about deciding who can enjoy something like a club, is that it means some people are left out. Some Christians say this about heaven. Because the Bible says that eternal life belongs only to believers, those who are not believers won't go to heaven.

That suggests that

1. Anyone who is not a Christian will not go to heaven.

2. You need to hear about Jesus and believe and obey his teaching in order to go to heaven.

This leaves us with the very difficult problem about those who have never heard about Jesus. What will happen to them when they die?

The *Bible* teaches that God will judge everyone according to what opportunities they were given to

Right: Or should clubs be for one sort of person only, like a single selection pack?

respond to God's love during their life. God is a loving, fair Judge, who never makes any mistakes. Does this mean that members of other faiths can go to heaven? What do you think?

Jesus taught that people who just pretended to be his followers, even calling themselves Christians, would not be in heaven. See *Matthew* 7:21.

In the Second World War, people called Nazis, in Germany, murdered millions of people, many of them Jews. Some Nazis said they were Christians, and were punishing the Jews for killing Jesus. How can anyone do something so horrible and expect a place in heaven? What do you think?

Part 6

Death itself

What's it like to die? That's a difficult question because anyone still alive hasn't experienced it. We imagine it as something very painful. In fact, today's modern medicines mean that people who are on the brink of death usually have little or no pain.

But in *Bible* times, there was very little available to reduce suffering, except perhaps some sour wine to make you drunk. A few herbs were available, too, but some had nasty side effects.

Just 60 years ago, even a visit to the dentist was a nightmare. People were employed to pin someone down to stop them struggling while the dentist worked – without anaesthetics.

Fortunately, those days are long past. We are given an anaesthetic if we have to have a tooth out. And people who are on the brink of death (terminally ill) are eased into death with powerful painkillers.

As you get older, you're likely to have been close to people or animals who die – maybe your grandparents, or your pet hamster. Of course you'll be very sad, and whether it's a person or animal, you'll miss them terribly.

One day, you might even have to sit next to someone as they die. That's very hard to do.

But what's really surprising is that seeing others die sometimes shows us that death isn't as terrible as we often think.

For instance, some people hear the dying person talking about an incredible light which they seem to see. Many dying people hold out their arms as if someone is welcoming them in a loving way. And most smile, as if something wonderful is happening to them.

All this shows that death can't be that bad. People who are dying rarely say anything, except perhaps to mention the wonderful light. But, we do hear accounts from people who did die and who, remarkably, came back to life for one reason or another.

What these people say about what happened is often very similar.

The next few pages describe their experiences.

When the police investigate a crime, they

talk about it...

You can only do this activity if there's a group of you. One of you should not take part. You'll understand why in a moment.

All but one of you should look at the picture above.

Now answer this simple question – what colour is the cat?

Tell the person who didn't see it.

Everyone should have said it is black and white. Each of you saw the cat in your own way, but you are all agreed about what its colours were.

The person who didn't see the picture has no reason not to believe what you say about it.

ask witnesses to describe what happened. Some details will differ, but largely people will see the same things.

Sometimes the things that have happened to us in the past affect how we see the world. For instance, I once taught a boy who always ducked when I went near him. I'd never even thought of hitting him, but he was used to being hit at home. He ducked whenever he saw an adult, to avoid being hit. Not everyone does this. Depending on what's happened to us in our lives, we interpret things differently.

So it's not surprising that there are slight differences in the way people describe what happened after they'd died – what's remarkable is how close their stories can be.

Left: Being close to someone who's dying is always moving – but it isn't always as sad or as terrible as you might think.

Right: The first death many people experience is that of a pet.

Part 7

Life in heaven

This picture of Mars is based on pictures sent back to Earth by the space probes, so it's not a bad likeness. But some things aren't easy to show in a picture. We can't see from this how hot it is during the day — because Mars has no atmosphere to protect it from the Sun — or how bitterly cold it is at night.

for you to try...

Take a piece of paper and some pencils. Draw and colour a picture showing what the surface of the planet Mars looks like. Will there be craters? Dust? Clouds?
Is there water? An atmosphere? Are there roads and rivers? Towns? Is it hot or cold?
How will you show all these things in your picture?

Now here are some more questions. If there's a group of you, talk them through together.
How do you know what Mars is like? Have you ever been there? Has anyone ever been there? Or have you seen pictures of it? How much of what you drew is what you think Mars is like, or would like it to look? How much is provable?

So what has Mars got to do with heaven? Only this. You and I have never seen heaven. We haven't even seen pictures of it, except ones that show what some people think it looks like. No-one has ever taken a photograph of heaven, or sent us back rock samples.

But, as you will see, some people think they have seen heaven, and been sent back.

This happened to one of my friends.

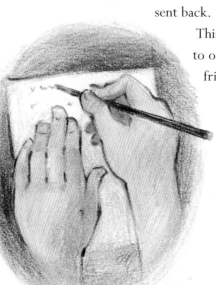

Above: An image based on something we haven't seen will come partly from our imagination, and partly from what we've been told.

Below: Satellite images of distant planets tell us what they're like.

Right: Some people believe they can describe a glimpse of heaven.

On three separate occasions my friend believes he ended up in heaven, but each time he was sent back.

On all three occasions he saw a house which he somehow knew was going to be his. He never saw any builders, but each time the house had been made a bit better. And he realised that when the house was finished, it would be time for him to stay.

The third time he went, everything looked more beautiful than ever and he even saw a most stupendous waterfall.

I'm sorry to say my friend has since died. I wonder if he's really gone where he always thought he would?

If we do go to a kind of heaven or paradise when we die, what would you hope to find there?

Part 8

Rick's journey to heaven

Rick was a happy, bright boy. He loved his mum and dad and his school. In fact, he just loved being alive. Then, one awful day, he became very ill. He was rushed to hospital with meningitis.

His temperature was very high, and he became delirious – that is, his brain became so hot he could only speak nonsense. Later, he couldn't remember any of this.

But one thing Rick did remember. He saw, all round him, an incredible light. And he felt himself moving up through it.

Below him, lying in a hospital bed, he could see a boy. With a shock, he realised it was himself. He couldn't understand how he could be lying down there and looking down at himself at the same time. Clustered round the bed were his mum and dad, a doctor and a nurse. The doctor was trying to do something to him, and he almost laughed, because he knew it was useless.

Then, he was moving again. He couldn't see the bed any more. Instead, in front of him, was a huge net. He said afterwards that it was like the ones they have on army assault courses. He realised he had to climb over it. There were other children there, too, and as he watched he saw several climb over the top and disappear.

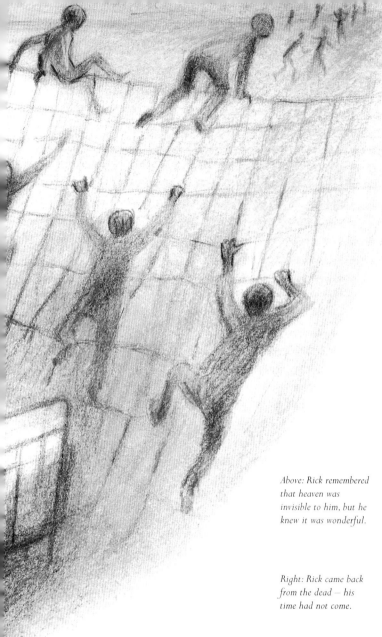

Above: Rick remembered that heaven was invisible to him, but he knew it was wonderful.

Right: Rick came back from the dead – his time had not come.

Rick knew that somewhere over there was something truly wonderful and he longed to be there. He started scrambling up the net. At first, it seemed very easy, then it got harder and harder. Other children overtook him, climbed over, and disappeared. He couldn't understand why he was finding it so hard.

But at last he reached the top. He had swung half his body over when heard someone say, 'No, Rick, you can't come. It's not the

right time. Go back."

He was bitterly disappointed because he knew that whatever was there was wonderful. He hesitated, then continued to clamber over.

"No! You cannot come!" the voice insisted. Rick couldn't move forward at all. He was halfway over, yet he couldn't go any further. Something – he couldn't see what – was pushing him back.

With great reluctance, Rick stepped back over the net.

Suddenly he was awake. The doctor and nurse were leaning over him, and to his right he could see his mum, crying. His dad looked like he'd been crying too.

"That was close," the doctor said.

It was only later, when he read about other peoples' reports of dying and coming back, that he understood what had happened.

That day he'd died, but had come back.

And later, when he'd recovered from the meningitis, his mum confirmed what he remembered. He had been dead for just a few seconds, but the doctor had managed to bring him back to life.

Part 9

Judgement

Most people who have 'near death' experiences, get no further than a glimpse of what might be heaven. But the few who have got further than this also seem to agree about what they saw. Very quickly after 'arriving', they feel that they are being judged.

They say that past events, when they did good or evil, flash before them. They hear voices speaking on their behalf – as if there was some unseen court trying them.

Of the hundreds of cases like this which have been written about, all but one have reported that next, they became aware that their misdeeds had been forgiven. Most also saw a bright light which they believe must be either Jesus or God.

But one man reported being taken to see hell. Later, when he came round, he said he couldn't actually remember what it looked like, except it wasn't nice. It was made clear to him that he was being sent back to life, but that if he didn't sort himself out, he would end up there.

How much all this really happened is impossible to say. But, many of these people hadn't heard of other people's experiences. These experiences are too similar and happen to too many people for everyone to have made them up.

Below: Many people's experiences have included being 'weighed' against the things they did in their lives.

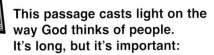

from the Bible...

This passage casts light on the way God thinks of people. It's long, but it's important:

Do you not know that God's kindness is meant to lead you to repentance? But by your hard and impenitent heart, you are storing up wrath for yourself on the day of wrath when God's righteous judgement will be revealed. For he will render to every man according to his works: to those who by patience in well-doing seek for glory and honour and immortality, he will give eternal life; but for those who are factious and do not obey the truth, but obey wickedness, there will be wrath and fury. There will be tribulation and distress for every human being who does evil, the Jew first and also the Greek, but glory and honour and peace for everyone who does good, the Jew first and also the Greek. For God shows no partiality.

All who have sinned without the law will perish without the law, and all who have sinned under the law will be judged by the law. For it is not the hearers of the law who are righteous before God, but the doers of the law who will be justified. When Gentiles who have not the law do by nature what the law requires, they are a law to themselves, even though they do not have the law. They show that what the law requires is written on their hearts, while their conscience also bears witness and their conflicting thoughts accuse or perhaps excuse them on that day when, according to my gospel, God judges the secrets of men by Christ Jesus.

Romans 2:4–16, Revised Standard Version

for you to try...

Some of the words in the passage are quite hard. Look at the list below.

On a piece of scrap paper, write down the numbers 1 to 19 first. These are for the difficult words. Next to each number, write the letter that goes with the word's definition.

If you match them all correctly, the letters will spell out a message.

1. Repentance	**A)** Shown to be right
2. Impenitent	**D)** Just; right with God
3. Sin	**E)** Not being sorry
4. Distress	**E)** Favouritism
5. Righteous	**E)** Opposing
6. Despise	**G)** Anger
7. Wickedness	**H)** Decision
8. Partiality	**I)** Die
9. Glory	**L)** Wrong doing
10. Conscience	**L)** Sorrow
11. Factious	**N)** Evil
12. Justified	**O)** Hate
13. Gentiles	**O)** Sense of right or wrong
14. Conflicting	**R)** Non-Jews
15. Render	**R)** Give in return
16. Perish	**T)** Great sadness
17. Wrath	**U)** Self-seeking
18. Judgement	**W)** Being sorry
19. Tribulation	**Y)** Heavenly splendour

Part 10

What are heaven and hell really like?

Jesus said more about heaven and hell than anyone else in the Bible. *Jesus pictured heaven as a house. Look up John 14:2 in your* Bible

Above: Young people's drawings often show heaven 'up there'.

talk about it...

Lots of people have come up with their own ideas about hell. If you are on your own, think your way through these questions. If you are in a group, discuss them together.

Do you think there is such a place as hell? If not, why not? If you feel there is, talk (or think) about what you imagine hell's like.

Perhaps they didn't realise that when the body dies, the central nervous system fails too, and therefore it's impossible to feel anything physical after death.

Later, people began to think of heaven as being a paradise, like the garden of Eden. Hell was being locked out of that garden.

After Jesus, people's ideas changed again. Jesus taught that heaven is being with him and accounting for your actions, while hell is being separated from him.

In the middle ages, heaven was 'up there' in the clouds (and some people even thought the stars were heaven's lights on!) and hell was 'down there'. People thought the devil was a fallen angel who tempted them into sin.

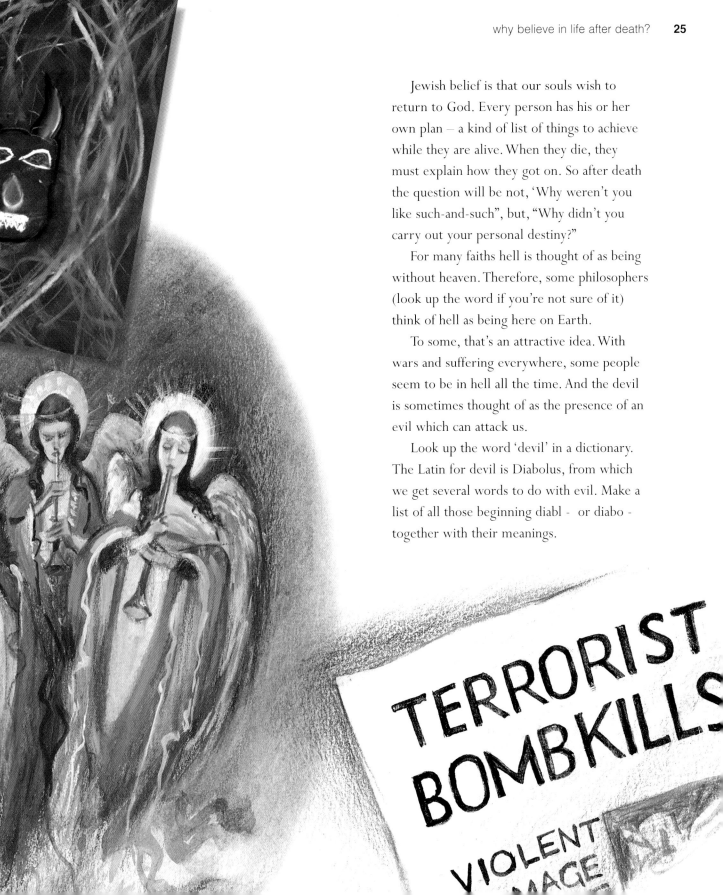

Jewish belief is that our souls wish to return to God. Every person has his or her own plan – a kind of list of things to achieve while they are alive. When they die, they must explain how they got on. So after death the question will be not, 'Why weren't you like such-and-such", but, "Why didn't you carry out your personal destiny?"

For many faiths hell is thought of as being without heaven. Therefore, some philosophers (look up the word if you're not sure of it) think of hell as being here on Earth.

To some, that's an attractive idea. With wars and suffering everywhere, some people seem to be in hell all the time. And the devil is sometimes thought of as the presence of an evil which can attack us.

Look up the word 'devil' in a dictionary. The Latin for devil is Diabolus, from which we get several words to do with evil. Make a list of all those beginning diabl - or diabo - together with their meanings.

Part 11

But did they really experience it?

Using the experience of other people can be unreliable. But what if what they say sounds right? Too many people have described the light, the net, the 'tunnel', the judgement and the beauty of heaven.

It's impossible for all those people in all those different parts of the world to have made it all up. Isn't it?

Haven't you had things happen to you you're convinced must have occurred. But which in reality didn't?

For instance, when I was a boy, there was a huge mirror. I strongly remember opening the front of it once and finding a room behind it. I am positive it happened. I can remember the size of the room, that it was dusty and dark.

I never managed to open that mirror and find the room ever again. I now know there was no such room. As an adult, I even took the mirror off the wall when I had to clear furniture from the house. Even though I know for sure that there was no room there, my mind still remembers that odd little room.

*Right: It's possible to 'know' some thing has happened which you also know **can't** have occurred.*

left: Almost everyone who has had a near death experience reports a dazzling, blinding light.

Supposing the near death experiences which people have had are like that. Suppose there's a medical reason.

For instance, when we die, our heart stops and our lungs stop, and no oxygen can reach the brain. Maybe the great light and everything after that happens because the brain is starved of oxygen?

Then everyone would experience the same things because, in that sort of situation, everyone's brains would always work in exactly the same way.

So perhaps all the evidence from people who have gone through near death experiences might not have happened at all. We can't be sure.

Except for one thing. Shortage of oxygen might explain the light, the net-like obstacle, the tunnel and the light at the other end. It might even explain the beauties people see when they get 'there'.

But one thing it can't explain is why people find themselves being 'judged'. Some people say it's a bit like being weighed on a weighing scale to see how much good you've done. Could that bit really be caused by oxygen shortage?

What do you think?

1 Things aren't always what they seem.

2 We can learn by experience.

3 If there's no life after death, it doesn't matter what we do on Earth.

4 Jesus rose again after he died – and there are lots of eyewitness accounts to prove it.

5 The Bible tells us there is life after death.

6 When we see people die, many seem to smile at someone welcoming them.

7 We know about heaven from human 'probes' – who have had 'near-death' experiences.

8 Some witnesses, like Rick, have actually died and come back to life. They report a beautiful light.

9 Some 'near-death' witnesses feel they are being judged.

10 Many people believe that 'heaven' is being with God and 'hell' is being without God.

11 Scientific explanations for experiences do not account for judgement.

ISBN 1-85608-381-0

Designed by
THE BRIDGEWATER BOOK COMPANY LTD
Designer Andrew Milne

Write to:
HUNT & THORPE
Deershot Lodge, Park Lane, Ropley,
nr. Alresford, Hampshire SO24 0BE, UK

Hunt & Thorpe is a name used under licence by
Paternoster Publishing, PO Box 300,
Kingstown Broadway, Carlisle, CA3 0QS, UK

A CIP catalogue record for this book
is available from the British Library.

Printed in Singapore